*the wine tasted sweeter
in the paper cups*

the wine tasted sweeter in the paper cups

love poems

carlos carrio

KONSTELLATION
PRESS

Konstellation Press
San Diego
Konstellationpress.com

Cover design: Scarlet Willette
Editor: Cornelia Feye

SBN-13: 978-0998748238
ISBN-10: 0998748234

i love you as certain dark things are to be loved,
in secret, between the shadow and the soul

pablo neruda
one hundred love sonnets: xvii

.

Contents

i made love to god today
the end is never clear
the scratches on my arm
my heart was soft and blue
i know you think of me
the fog of passion
i gaze at your feet like an icon
the soap caresses her
in the sacred
her leg painted with scars
not for sex but for soul
my heart always returns to you
i stared at the moon in reverence
where are we to go
you saturate my consciousness
she would break his heart

~ i ~
madness

a terrorist love
love gone never seems to depart
tonight i sit in a godless hole
you're the lifetime i want to begin
between sadness and fear
let me sleep
the burnt scent of your love
the acidic drip of your kiss
the evening melancholy is a whore
awkward romance

the is purgatory
every day I die
the kind of pain love demands
the butterflies have awakened
emptiness

~ iv ~
longing

you are my metaphor
i thought i lost you
i sit alongside orpheus
the fog of memory
it feels like I'm losing you
sundays at seven
the sandals slap your feet
picture behind a picture
she looked like you
farewells are like grenades
farewells are like grenades (the next night)
do you think of me
easy silence
sweet melancholy
do you remember
my irrational heart
the eve before thanksgiving
she was not mine
i miss you
when the morning arrives

drowning above water
last night he dreamed
if I forget you
dance of desire and fear
the long winter
the sensation of your leg

Dedication

pg

~ i ~

tenderness

the wine tasted sweeter in the paper cups

the wine tasted sweeter in the paper cups
your legs like a feather across my lap
a minute became an hour when you leaned on me
something about staring at the water
from the brooklyn side

the breeze hardly a whisper
the twilight sun embraced us
i was cooled by your warm breath
as we sat on the bench stealing kisses
under your sweater that covered our heads

the sun fell asleep
the moon awakened
it greeted us with goodbye
and the nighttime gently kissed us
as we held hands and then let go

sometimes our hands touch

coffee with her is how we make love

sometimes our hands touch

sharing stories told before

we laugh and smile again

the silence always comes too soon

to seek our empty cups

i cry behind the smile sad to let go

looking forward to my next coffee with her

when she calls

when she calls he slips into her like a warm bath

the break in his heart filled by her velvet voice

his sad eyes staring at a faraway dream

i touched her arm

her face glowed like an angel as she cried
i yearned to wipe the tears
instead i touched her arm and made her smile
that was enough for today

flower petals falling

she sleepwalked for several years but didn't know

every night she died a restless sleep

every morning a walk on the clouds

looking down at the abyss in awe and terror

as the breeze caressed her breasts

consoled her with the memory of her lover's

    hands

 from a gentle and truthful sleep

she awakened at the sound of flower petals

    falling

these sad eyes are yours

these sad eyes are yours

they hunger to see you bare

the face of a scarred angel no longer self conscious

i've kissed those wounds a thousand times

and breathed on them as a ritual

they gaze at the marks of the broken humanity

> you carry in a crying heart hidden under that
>
> wide smile

no one can see the tears i wipe away in the dark

what is more precious than your sighs

i listen to you breathe as i stare out the window and
    wonder
what can i say that is more precious than your
    sighs
the cadence of your gasps and the stillness of each
    pause is more angelic than the words of my
    unclean lips
my silence is a song i give to you
a gift that speaks the lines and lulls you to sleep
your eyes hum the refrain and our tears turn the
    pages
as i pull up a chair and touch your face

when all that remains is fear and sorrow

when all that remains is fear and sorrow and the
    light has dimmed but our souls yearn for the
    other
sometimes all we can give
sometimes all we need
is silence and the love naked bodies understand

.

~ ii ~

passion

the light and the shadow dance and fight

the silence was worse than the screaming, a language
    i didn't understand
the guttural sounds came fast and furious and i knew
    she either hated my guts or was madly in love
fluent yesterday today a tongue of a different kind
the eyes the mouth and the heavy sighs become the
    subject the verb the whole damn sentence
passion one day fury the next
the light and the shadow dance and fight
i pulled her hair she grabbed my shirt
i kissed her lips she traced my ear
racing hearts identic rhythms whether we scream or
    love
silence the only sound that makes sense
her feet rest on the dash board as she inhales slow
    and deep
the quirky socks and paisley shirt that laid on the
    floor next to mine now a security blanket that
    shields her from fear and shame

reentry to real life is always painful

let me be the one tonight

let me be the one tonight
the whisper that makes you lean
the finger that strokes your face
the secret that makes you smile
the touch that makes you sigh
the eyes that pull you in
the puzzle that eludes you

who knows where the wind will blow
how this journey will unfold
and cares not what we think
tomorrow a mystery
come my caramel darkness
hide under our shadow
let's be broken together

i promise my voice when you call
my love when you fear
my heart when you doubt

my touch when you ache

my gaze when you need to be reminded of your

    beauty

and a glass of cabernet

the ring on your finger

like the train i can hear in the distance
here it comes i can feel it the nighttime
feel my chest burn where are you gentle moon
you have gone slowly leaving this growing
never ending teasing pile of kindling
which multiplies the heated clouds raising
the temperature of my heart and i
wonder why are you not with me tonight

the ring on your finger is not mine it
weighs heavy on your heart this small piece of
social contract it can be removed so
gently yet causing a flesh wound that burns
but if you walk with me and breathe with me
my ring of love will heal you this evening

my mocha queen

what do you see with your large eyes my mocha
    queen
do they throb with the beauty of the world
    or do they bulge with its horrors
what heavy thoughts fill your mind today
    your neck can barely hold its weight

how i wish to kiss that long neck my mocha queen
    while your flowing hair fills my mouth
your waist so thin and strong
    it bares the center of your soul
so comfortable as you sit

where are you going my mocha queen
take me to your silence
let me hold on to you
for my useless legs aimlessly journey

the elixir is in my mouth

your narcissism ties up the wrists of the soft and pink
    girl
never enough to kill her just enough to enslave her
and all i can do is watch

and when she escapes you fall in love again
until that brilliant mind awakens and you mercilessly
    beat her and spit at me
the man in whose arms you collapsed and cried and
    loved
and all i can do is watch

your stage four anxiety overwhelms the
    loneliness
but remission comes when we meet each other again
    for the first time

your remedy writes these words

the elixir is in my mouth

close your eyes

show me your veins

let me untie the girl in you

snow as lover

the beauty of the snow is not its precious whiteness

its beauty comes in covering the ugliness beneath

like the lover who climbs onto me and hides my

    wounds

 a generous and merciful lover is

    this snow

whose silence whispers to me and all i hear is the

    ticking of life

the sound of my heart melting

    knowing it will soon be gone

don't leave me

but for the moment i fall into it

play with it

am covered by it

embracing the beautiful season i don't want to end

just below the heart

you're more on my mind than in my bones today

more thoughts than aches

but there you are ever simmering

just below the heart

hair dark like the secrets we keep

mouth strong like the whiskey we drink

your passion drips on to me

my blood pours into you

    as i wipe away your tears and bring you into

    the moment

swagger tall and confident

i love those boots you wear

your words mesmerize them

tease comfort bewitch them

but i've kissed those tangerine lips and held your

    quivering hips

your face in my blood

my kingdom for a kiss

a tongue that cuts

our bodies entwined and then i awake

to see your face in my blood

snow falling in the morning

silence

i look for you

this unattainable love

this race without end

this gasp for air

the fire you lit

the fire you lit ever simmers

and i fear one day one moment it will consume me

but i wonder do you burn the same

absolution in each other's arms

the thirst of a man

water in his hands

seeps through the fingers

the pain of absence lingers

but lives in memory

restless menagerie

she the priestess who feeds

the bread his soul needs

moonlight lovers

immortal confessors

he knows she knows they know

no other place to go

to find absolution

but in each other's arms

she hides my wounds

the leaves lay upon the way

    like golden sheets

the dirt unseen her legs they wrap

    the spider web

my wounds hid under her gaze

    blanket of love

i made love to god today

i made love to god today

she loved fiercely extravagantly recklessly

and then rested smiling with guileless innocence

between scylla and charybdis lay i

shot with the arrow of eros

helpless in orgasmic joy and pain

how else can it be when one fucks a deity

the end is never clear

my eyes blink as the sand rises swirling all around

i disappear into the dust devil

a hiding place for my secrets where the wine never

     ends and the tears never dry

the push and pull of you and me forms and heals the

     scars

your hand is mine my breath is yours our thoughts

     crash in the air

raining in this desert place

where the horizon encircles us and the end is never

     clear

confident and frightened bold and foolish we search

     for the unknown

hold each other with one hand

reach for mystery with the other

kiss me quick

let's disappear for a moment

the sand is beginning to swirl again

the scratches on my arm

i saw the scratches on my arm and knew this
    morning was different
from the daily rituals filled with mundanity and the
    cycle of ordinariness threading our lives
as the light of day opened my eyes i could still feel
    your nails enter me as i entered you
and for a twilights moment a dark quiet space
    opened to the sound of your teeth biting and
    my flesh ripping
i smile at the cuts across the veins an ecstatic pain
    knowing my skin slept with you under your nails

my heart was soft and blue

yesterday my heart was soft and blue

not soft like a meaningless affirmation

    or soft like a hanging twig

but soft as the soul marinating in the waters of life

    that refreshes my tired and dusty body

yesterday my heart was soft and blue

not blue as in sadness that weighs one down

    or blue as the sound of a saxophone in a smoky

    room

but blue as the color of a man

    who walks with the sun on his back

yesterday my heart was soft and blue

the type of softness a man yearns to bend his leathery

    soul

the type of blueness a man craves at the whisper of

    his lover's voice

i know you think of me

when all those around are asleep

and the sounds of the night are dimmer

when the lights of the stars grow louder

and the silence increases its simmer

when all the pages are read

and all the lies have been said

as your mind is resting in bed

with your hands crossing your chest

i know you think of me

the fog of passion

the fog of passion escapes as i open the door to the
moment where we will soon be
the mist of your presence fills the room with white
clouds which envelop me as i enter

and i inhale

like a boxer who bobs and weaves before the fight
which titillates and terrifies

and i inhale

as the anticipation pierces my lungs dries my mouth
fills my heart with passion blood
ready to burst and spray the walls
i anxiously pace and wait for the knock staring at the
bed where you will soon lay
but all is calm and easy when i see your face and we smile

i gaze at your feet like an icon

i gaze at your feet

    like an icon that calls me to worship

i approach your feet

    like gravity pulling me into destiny

i touch your feet

    like a relic and tremble within

i hold your feet

    like a chalice cup of my salvation

i kiss your feet

    like a baptism of sweat tears and tongue

the soap caresses her

it grabs me five minutes in

when the lukewarm water turns hot and the steam

    swirls round my face

when the shampoo runs down my back and the

lather

    embraces my thighs

as i rest my face on the cool wet tile

it is she who holds my mind

i feel her drip upon my feet as the soap caresses her

    breasts

i taste her hair in my mouth but i never see her face

she always looks away in this bittersweet memory

    rewind

as i rest my face on the cool wet tile

it is she who holds my mind

in the sacred

i hear the candles flickering

i see the gold cross glimmering

i smell the incense burning

but my thoughts return to you

the morning light embraces

the red curtain traces

most sacred of all spaces

but my thoughts return to you

as i sit on this pew

strength of mind i thought i knew

i could not be askew

but my thoughts return to you

i hear the organ roaring

i see the people rising

i feel the music soaring

but my thoughts return to you

my knees continue praying
"remove this pain!" i'm pleading
my tears like rivers flowing
but my thoughts return to you

her leg painted with scars

i held her leg painted with scars
she traced the wound on my hand
humming a tune looking away
she must let me go again

that old familiar film replayed
laughter scene one
whisper scene two
kiss farewell fade in three

"i'll drive you crazy!" she said
but crazy becomes calm
calm becomes passion
she pushed unable to let go

i was broken that night
she felt it in her arms
"how do my tears taste?" i asked
come break my heart again

not for sex but for soul

once again

lay withme

notforsex

butforsoul

hold my hand

be with me

take me there

oh my love

to the place

where i live

many come

but few stay

the address

is displayed

my body

visited

sojourners

all tourists

who see me

who touch me

yet wonder

where i am

but you know

how to go

to the place

of my soul

a space that's

familiar

it's a street

we both live

are the lights

on i see

are you alone

again my love

may i come

and visit

to the place

of your soul

my heart always returns to you

it's the first time i've seen you since all hell broke
   loose
you look beautiful in that black dress with the white
   sweater
will i ever recover
can i ever return
what can distance do
is time anything
what does it matter when my heart always returns to
   you

i stared at the moon in reverence

i stared at the moon in reverence last night
its beauty seized me the way you did
when you wore the summer dress that warm saturday
    night

we're not children of the sun but souls of the moon
gently healing each other's wounds that fester during
    the day beneath the masks we wear

come with me into the shadow where darkness
    abounds
infused with the sounds of breathlessness and the
    moisture of our love

stillness comes when i lift the burdens off your
    shoulders
they carry the weight of loyalty and responsibility
a pendulum you fiercely embrace

for now i love you the only way i can

as moonlight reflects off the river

as a breeze blows in the garden

as raindrops bounce on the sidewalk

where are we to go

if love is knowing and to be known then where are we
    to go

who knows you like i know you

i know you as deeply as the cactus knows the sun

as the snow dances with the wind burning and
    wetting your face

like the fish that puffs its lips and knows the water

i know your lips wet and they puff my lips

i know you

if love is knowing and to be known then where are we
    to go

who knows me like you know me

like the mountaintops kiss the clouds

like the spider feels the web as it comes out of her
    and entraps me

like the chocolate milk you pour into my mouth

you know me

if love is knowing and to be known then where are we

    to go

who will drink you like i drink you

with my body and soul

who will taste me like you taste me

with your touch and heart

where are we to go

you saturate my consciousness

it's time for me to journey for a while

your love saturates my consciousness

i've never experienced this

my soul seems to drown in you

understand that sometimes

i must pull away

tend to my heart

catch my breath

return

kiss

she would break his heart

when she kissed him as she got into the car

when she called him on the second night

when she wrinkled her nose

when she laid on the sofa

when she rested on his lap

when he entered her and she said "damn!"

when they held each other in bed

when she covered his eyes and never opened hers

he knew she would break his heart

~ iii ~

madness

a terrorist love

i fear my love for you

it is a terrorist love

a passion so all encompassing it can only lead to

     destruction

something will die

i am a lamb to the slaughter

a moth to the flame

a hungry man who follows the smell of food

wherever it may lead whatever it may cost

i am powerless

the irrational is reasonable

what is wrong is right

what is poison is eucharist

and i take body and blood of it

as it drips down my neck

amen

love gone never seems to depart

i stare at the blank page with drink in one hand pen
    in another
needing to write to free the demons and save my soul
 it hits me like a tsunami
 awareness toward the probable
is it possible there's no turning back
have we walked through the door of no return
welded beyond the tearing of merged souls
i slowly sip the glass
wipe my lips and mustache
as the whiskey warms my throat
love gone never seems to depart

tonight i sit in a godless hole

tonight i sit in a godless hole

drenched in the sludge of misery

as the tar of loneliness pours

my chest torn open

heart shredded

blood oozing from the ripped flesh

you have burned me

the acrid smell of your love

chokes the room

i'm suffocating

covered by the ashes left behind

from the explosion of my soul

paralyzed in this hell

blistering from the acid of your memory

desperately looking at the phone that will never ring

you're the lifetime i want to begin

you're the lifetime i now want to begin
i'm the problem which you struggle to solve
you're the spice that my tongue so desires
i'm the taste you are trying to spit out
you're the magnet to whom i've surrendered
i'm the pull you so desperately push
you're the subject the center of my play
i'm the object of death in your story

you knock me down then quickly run to brush
the dirt off myself who you gingerly
hold in your hands as a wounded brown bird
you kiss feed and place in your breast pocket
which keeps me near your heart but prevents me
from spreading my wings and flying away

between sadness and fear

the back and forth of sadness and fear is madness

a sea of sand quick and ever sinking

i grasp the air and reach for hope

the ground shifts an eternal abyss

like a shark i move so i don't die

a scarf of lilies is laid on me

but today a glimmer a light peeks

the tears and waters merge as i cough

let me sleep

when i sleep
i whisper
rest my muse

when i wake
and my mind
clears the fog
you appear

i beseech
go away
deja vu
you return

what is this
wicked curse
you hexed me
enchanted

like a drum
bolero
incantation
cruel sorrow

once again
you appear
long for thee
will it end

my heart falls
my core aches
as i gaze
at your smile

and whisper
let me sleep
vexing muse
till the morn

the burnt scent of your love

the fire in my heart ever burns
the wind blows the flame flickers
but it never quenches
like the scar on your thigh
my heart a hardened wound
the sparks dance in my mind
you have burned me
and the smoky scent of your love
wakes me walks me sleeps me

the acidic drip of your kiss

the highway of death isopropyl in the air

the stick of the needle brings me to this moment

where my blood and your blood

swirl as a dance of flamenco and guitar

incense rises bittersweet scent of my flesh

as the veins darken by the burn from

the acidic drip of your kiss

yet i smile with bliss unable to foresee the crash

over the bodies of men with darkened veins and

    blissful smiles

the evening melancholy is a whore

its sunday night

the dark cloud of melancholy is

    falling fast

an all consuming shadow blinds me

a weight on my chest

salty tears to the taste

this bitter whore of medicine

the silent phone

no texts received

how i long to sleep a merciful death

but sunday night will come again tomorrow

awkward romance

i speed north up the parkway to get away faraway

left her south in a box to bury it forget it

my dream sleeps deep so i lower the door creak

but she always reawakens hastens and i let her back

    in

our dance our stance our awkward romance

    where lilies never die neither she nor i

as we try to untie the goodbye

that never sticks this brick of lies

the crickets sing me lull me a choir of angels tonight

warm me console me o evening light

it drips this crypt this hole in my chest

the blood on the ground can be washed quick

the pain is constrained by many a drink

she clenches revenges my warm heart in

her gorgeous damn hands with pink nails

    the left one with the ring

which scratches malpractice my face with words

the talk with crossed arms never matches her walk

she heals me steels me with a kiss

then cuts me shreds me once again

with that smile wide as a mile which she knows

    drives me wild and i'll

never break free from she

for i have forgiven thee many times before

so i drive north up the parkway to get away faraway

from the pain this causes this cross is

so heavy to bear but i stare

and miss her insist her to hold me once again

but i fear very near as she jumps off the merry go

    round

it'll be my turn to lay down in the box

this is purgatory

so this is purgatory
between heaven and hell am i

may i sip of you
just enough to satisfy
for if i imbibe too much the passions overwhelm my
    equilibrium

may i sip of you
but alas with one drop i am intoxicated again
with you heaven
with you hell
without you hell
this is purgatory

every day i die

every day i die a thousand deaths remembering

holding your hand

kissing your lips

tasting your thighs

every day i die a thousand deaths because reality is

fantasy

and fantasy is a cut

every day i die a thousand deaths as i bury myself

once again in this sisyphean grief

the kind of pain love demands

somewhere between my navel and chest

on the left side of the highway north of memory a

    fire burns

slow and tenacious withering of a past presence

the once large magical bonfire is now a smoldering

light in the rearview

it is my lover extending her gift of pain

the kind that love demands it chars and creates

    new skin

therapeutic burning scars the heart

a work of art compelling and free

the butterflies have awakened

the butterflies have awakened
they flutter violently passionately
no space to spread their wings
crashing into each other
downward madness
screaming in silent wail
"where are you?"

emptiness

i choose nothing
because emptiness is more bearable than the
    constant reminder of love unattainable
let us walk away for both our sakes

~ iv ~

longing

you are my metaphor

one day we will be family

as you leave the shoes at the door and rest your

    weary legs across my lap

i massage your tired feet and smile

listening to the complaints of the day

you love to talk and i love to watch your lips move

it only lasts a few minutes before i kiss you

then your shoulders drop and that hard body softens

the one you've sculpted from the hurts of life and

    the battles in your mind

even wonder woman wants to feel loved

round and round it goes

but when the arrow points to our linked souls your

    hand quickly spins the wheel while the other

    holds a new book

it's easier to escape in the pages of knowledge than to

    stand in the place of vulnerability

for this you know but it's not what you want

denial is your virtue

pain the pillow that comforts

you fight windmills to avoid intimacy

"how can this be good if it brings so much pleasure?"

    your suspicious mind asks

but it does and i do and we do

tilt back your head and lay down

rest your swirling thoughts

unfurl your frightened heart

place your arms over your head and close your eyes

i love to hear you sigh

i have kissed you my butterfly

but you always return to the cocoon

it is night and my fingers crave to touch your wings

but you fly away from my open hand

the only way to hold you

gently loosely

how i wish to stroke your hair and whisper my words

for i am your poet and you are my metaphor

i thought i lost you

you stared at your shoes when i told you

about my love and you assured me

"i will dance with thee as you lead us

down into dante's spiral of passion"

you've fed me cherries with two wet fingers

dripping on my beard on your moist thighs

we spoke in whispers under warm shadows

i leaned and rested on your shoulder

you said to meet you tomorrow at eight

i said to meet me thursday at nine

you fear i am beginning to forget

i fear you are no longer interested

you laughed at my jokes and it warmed me

held my hand and it strengthened me

closed your eyes as we loved but you warned me

came in your mouth and you drank me

cried in my arms and it changed me

slept on my chest and it silenced me

screamed in my face and it frightened me

i thought i lost you and i did

until you called and i fell in love again

i sit alongside orpheus

the silence is deafening since you left me
the quiet after a storm leaves a path of
    destruction
now i sit alongside orpheus
among the debris singing the hymns of the dreadful
    night

the fog of memory

staring out the window the cars drive by

smell of coffee in the air fills my lungs

hypnotized by the falling leaves i reach

but the glass stops me

cold morning air held at bay by denim shirt and

    towel on my shoulder

the fog of memory rolls in again

as i stand in the lonesome draw thinking of you

the sizzle of bacon awakens my senses

hands still dripping from the dishes washed

like phantom pain from an amputated arm

i feel the throbbing of your presence

in my bowels sliced open by your farewell

the bleak heavy mist darkens my vision

step by step i go walking round blind

the fog of memory rolls in again

as i stand in the lonesome draw thinking of you

it feels like i'm losing you

it feels like i'm losing you
sand through my fingers slowly disappears
what remains are the grains of memories and
    the ache in my chest

oh how i would miss the tilt of your head when we
    kiss
the moisture of your hair with my sweat
the heat of your breath on my face
the tips of my fingers touching your nipples

oh how i would miss that sweet
    awkwardness of your intimacy
the hesitant admissions of your love
the cautious openings of your heart
the part you keep hidden from others and share with
    me in silence before you run away again

your soft and pink enswirls me today

it comes and goes like you and all i can do is write

these words

it feels like i'm losing you and i want to die

sundays at seven

sundays at seven remind me of you

or was it eight

when i would call or you would call

making promises we couldn't keep

until reality disrupted our dreams

you drinking wine on the roof me walking the streets

i laugh at your silly stories then silence on the phone

sundays at seven remind me of you

or was it eight

well

it doesn't matter now

does it

the sandals slap your feet

sitting by the river at four o'clock

water splashing against the wall

heat rising from the sidewalk

wrapped in the afternoon haze

i close my eyes and feel the sweat

arms dripping

shirt dampening

and then the sound of flip flops from a distance

    coming closer

i smile thinking of you

with your long dress short strides and hard walk

    as the sandals slap your feet

feet which i've held in my hands which i've caressed

    with my face which i've kissed a thousand times

i open my eyes as she passes by

it wasn't you it was the sound of you

and i keep smiling wondering where are you

    right now

what are you doing right now

picture behind a picture

i have a picture behind a picture which no one can
    see
an image i hide precious to me
when i look at the picture in front of the picture i do
    so smilingly
a clown's smile hiding the tears for thee
sometimes during upheavals i grab to rid the picture
    behind the picture
but her face is too lovely for me to free
i don't know why i keep the picture behind the
    picture
for it breaks my heart to know that she is a memory a
    a reality that will not grow
yet at times i am warmed by the picture behind the
    picture
her vulnerable face whispers "love"
for she had told me so

she looked like you

i saw a woman that looked like you

my heart skipped

my mouth dried

the hair was yours

the coquettish walk

the form fitting clothes

the longest three seconds of my life

my stomach tightened

chest ready to burst

i wanted to embrace you

to smell you

to kiss you

on the fourth second i saw it wasn't you

but a woman who looked like you

and i became very sad

farewells are like grenades

she lay on the bed fully clothed
staring at the ceiling fan mesmerized as it swirled
    round and round
ignoring her child's footsteps in the background
with eyes dazed like a soldier caught in the
concussion
    wave
the text she read blew her back into numbness
farewell, like an inverse grenade, exploded out of her
    stomach

farewells are like grenades (the next night)

she lay on the bed fully clothed
staring at the ceiling fan mesmerized as it swirled
    round and round
ignoring her child's footsteps in the background
with eyes dazed like a soldier caught in the
concussion
    wave
the text she read blew her back into numbness
farewell, like an inverse grenade, exploded out of her
    stomach

the next night she lay on the bed naked
staring at the fan thinking of the man
as her husband climbed on her

do you think of me

i sit in the quiet trying to forget

but visions of us crash in my head

today we kiss in the corridor

who are you whom i fear and want so near

do you think of me when you're fucking him

like i think of you when i'm fucking her

easy silence

it matters not the time that passes by
the multitude of distractions engaged
the summersaults of psychotherapy
the number of meditations practiced
i miss you my friend deep soul intimate
our talks our walks our fingers touching
the strength we give to each other
the easy silence of our quiet love
and the sound of your hum as we kiss

sweet melancholy

tonight i sit alone with the sweet melancholy that
    breaks my heart
you have left me and touched me in ways dark and
    lovely
you will not return this i know but your soul remains
you are there i am here we are one
you are here i am there we are one

do you remember

do you remember sitting in the park

do you think back at the first kiss

do you whisper my name in the shower

do you think of me when you touch yourself

do you yearn to rest your legs on my lap

do you tempt to text me when our song plays

do you smile thinking of grapes and giggles

do you miss drinking my wine and leaning

do you touch your lips remembering mine

do you sense my hands when you look at yours

do you recall how we danced on 10th

do you long for my sad eyes

do you tremble at our deep throated abandon

do you wish we could hold hands again

do you feel the warmth of my jacket

do you smell the scent of my skin

do you feel my fingers through your hair

do you crave your body pulled into mine

do you stand on your toes to kiss me in your mind

do you reminisce our late night banter

do you see my face when you rest

do you taste the tears that streamed down for you

my irrational heart

no one else i will love my muse

the words flow from your raspy voice which vibrates

my irrational heart

it aches bleeds simmers to burst

as i see you in the mist of nothingness

dancing laughing laying with me

i wait the melancholy wait until nothing is

    something

until then no one else i will love my muse

the eve before thanksgiving

the eve before thanksgiving

a missed call from you last night and i wonder

were you sad in need of comfort

did you accidently press the button

perhaps one glass too many

i still smile when your name appears

intimate friends with wounded hearts are eternally

    bound

she was not mine

we held hands across the avenue

walked like the city was ours and it was at that

    moment

but she was not mine she never was

our fingers interlocked like a lover's chain

we kissed the perfect kiss and it was at that moment

but i was not hers i never was

i miss you

i miss you

your quirky smile

your hesitant touch

your ebullient spirit

your agnostic theism

your slow kisses

your coconut hair

your salty neck

your dark nipples

your strong hands

your long fingers

your chipped nails

your strong legs

your sultry dance

your firm hold

your ceaseless confidence

your mass confusion

your astounding strength

your abundant insecurities

your head spinning moodiness

your nymphic beauty

your endless doubts

your raspy voice

your hidden vulnerability

your momentary love

your piercing cry

when the morning arrives

when the morning arrives

my heart is left void by your absence

if the gods are kind i am filled by your touch your

    kiss

the weight of your body on mine

my face resting on your stomach rising and falling

but if the gods are jealous my hunger is appeased by

    the memory of your waist

the scent of your hair

the taste of your thighs

and the image of your open mouth

drowning above water

as the dark water glimmers and the cold covers my
    feet
the ground pulls me in and the silence seizes me
with every wave that washes away her face fades
and i sink deeper under the weight of my tears
disappearing piece by piece drowning above water
under the midnight light paralyzed in this place

last night he dreamed

last night he dreamed that he wouldn't dream of her

mantric meditation kept the memory awake

last night he dreamed of lying on his side

staring at a blank wall but she stared back

last night he dreamed of a peaceful sleep

that morning would come uninterrupted

but this was only a dream

ififorgetyou

if i forget you my love i will certainly have died

or my mind floats in the waters of the unconscious

where nothing exists except my hand holding your

    hand

what good is a hand without a memory

if i forget you my love the rose you hold disappears

    for i will no longer be me but another whom

    you've never met

dance of desire and fear

ambiguity and vacillation never bothered me

messages from your virgin spirit

the dance of desire and fear

touch me leave me come back again

but the absence of your presence and the presence of

   your distance always left me wondering if we

   were we or i was it

for you were thou and i was i in my mind

i was never thou to you

you refused to become i for me

i was an it and this broke my heart

if we are we in your eyes then i could see us in the

   darkness

but if you see that we cannot be i and thou

then the brightness of the darkness can never shine

this makes me sad

for you are the shadow of my soul

i am the dark spot in your eyes

and the moonlight cleanses our secret

the long winter

as i look into her eyes
i can feel the sunshine warm my face after the long
    winter of her absent touch
and i confess

when her intensity lessens
when her volume lowers
when her shoulders soften at the cautious touch of
    our fingertips
i fall deeper into her

she knows with every minute that passes
as we stand at the edge holding hands

i lean forward
she leans back
her eyes leap but her feet remain
and i wonder
as the tears fall

does she cry for the past or the unknown

the sensation of your leg

sometimes at night the sensation of your leg resting

    on mine overtakes me and a cascade of

    restlessness escapes

i furiously toss back and forth

soothed by the memory of my finger in your mouth

and the heat of your breath on my hand

Acknowledgements

Nick Samaras is the kind of poet and spiritual seeker I wish to emulate. His love of life, of mystery, of aesthetic is throbbing with restless fervency, abundant empathy, endless curiosity, and a broken heart. Every verse of every poem he writes sings this glorious melancholy. Thank you, Nick.

From the beginning of my fledgling poetry writing, Anupama Amaran (A. Anupama) has been an encourager of my work, a sage-like mentor in the tradition of the great seer. Her own writing – simmering with grace, texture, and passion for life – has been an inspiration to me. Thank you, Anu.

At our first meeting, Cornelia Feye envisioned a beautiful book, and spoke of it often, like a mantra. She graciously embraced my poems, treated them with utmost respect, and provided a gentle and discerning touch. What more can a writer want from a publisher? Thank you, Cornelia.

E. Ethelbert Miller's poems proclaim the essence of humanity, the sacredness of the ordinary, the blood of a people, the ecstasy of the soul. Loves, tears, justice, and hope dance in his words. A kid from The Bronx took a chance on a kid from The Bronx. Thank you, Mr. Miller.

If I were in a foxhole, I'd want the River Writers Circle to be with me. These are my friends, but more than that; they were my weekly drinking buddies, but more than that; my poetry and prose sisters and brothers, but more than that; they are the compassionate kindred souls who understand the poor words I use and the tears I shed express a deeper yearning, a deeper connection, and a deeper meaning of which I am unable to express in any other way. Thank you, River River Writers Circle.

The North County Writers' Community has become my West Coast creative space where I can craft my words and be affirmed, even when they sound more contrived than organic. It has not been easy to maintain the discipline of writing as I journeyed from New York City to San Diego. But with this wonderful, eclectic and profoundly vulnerable group, I've experienced nothing but love, encouragement, and lots of laughs. Thank you, North County Writers' Community.

carloscarriopoetry@gmail.com
twitter.com/carriopoetry
facebook: Carlos Carrio